COOKING WITH
HEINZ KETCHUP

SMITHMARK

INTRODUCTION

Special Recipe Makes Heinz Ketchup Most Popular

Every year Heinz U.S.A. sells the equivalent of more than one billion 14-ounce bottles of ketchup! That's more than four bottles each for *every* person in the United States. Furthermore, it's sold and enjoyed throughout the world . . . from Lisbon to Tibet. In the United Kingdom alone, our British affiliate sells an equivalent of more than 59 million 14-ounce bottles a year.

Producing such a premier product means following stringent quality standards and undertaking years of arduous planning and research before the tomatoes ever reach the factory. This tradition started in 1876 when Henry Heinz first developed his ketchup recipe using only the choicest tomatoes. Today color, flavor and consistency often vary among the many mass-produced crops, and as a result, Heinz researchers have developed special tomato varieties possessing rich flavor, attractive color and firm texture.

In addition to the product itself, its package has also made it a worldwide favorite. In the 19th century, homemakers purchased Heinz Ketchup because of its convenience and its unique octagonal package. Since then, the Heinz glass ketchup bottle has changed very little. Consumers have come to expect the familiar panelled bottle with the keystone label and neck band. And, according to packaging trade publications, the Heinz Ketchup bottle is viewed, with the Coke bottle, as the "classic container of all time."

In addition to packaging ketchup in glass, Heinz introduced the squeezable plastic ketchup bottle in 1983. Today, more ketchup is packaged in plastic than in glass, and plastic-packaged ketchup continues to take an increasingly larger share of the market. Heinz continued its leadership in packaging with the introduction of its PETE bottle – made out of the most recyclable plastic available. The bottle's breakthrough technology keeps the ketchup fresh and allows communities to recycle their empty bottles.

In the future, Heinz will continue to explore innovative packaging that addresses the needs of consumers and society. But one thing never changes: Henry Heinz' original full-bodied recipe continues to be the basis for Heinz Tomato Ketchup – a product enjoyed throughout the world.

CLB 2601
©1992 Colour Library Books Ltd, Godalming, Surrey, England.
©1992 H.J. Heinz Co.
All rights reserved.
This edition published in 1992 by
SMITHMARK Publishers Inc., 112 Madison Avenue, New York, NY 10016.
Printed and bound in Singapore.
ISBN 0 8317 3196 6

SMITHMARK books are available for bulk sales promotion and premium use. For details write or telephone the Manager of Special Sales, SMITHMARK Publishers Inc., 112 Madison Avenue, New York, NY 10016. (212) 532-6600.

MINESTRONE WITH TORTELLINI

Makes 13 cups

Nothing says "home cooking" like a pot of hearty soup on a chilly day.

1½ pounds Italian sausage (hot or regular)
1 cup chopped onions
2 cloves garlic, minced
1 can (46 oz) beef or chicken broth (about 6 cups)
1 can (16 oz) whole tomatoes, cut into bite-size
   pieces
1 cup Heinz Tomato Ketchup
¾ cup dry red wine
2 cups thinly sliced carrots
1 cup thinly sliced celery
2 cups sliced zucchini
7 to 9 oz meat or cheese-filled tortellini
Grated Parmesan cheese

1. In Dutch oven, brown sausage; drain excess fat.

2. Add onions and garlic, and sauté until tender.

STEP 2

3. Add broth, tomatoes, ketchup, wine, carrots and celery; simmer, covered, 30 minutes.

STEP 3

4. Add zucchini and tortellini; simmer, covered 25 to 30 minutes.

STEP 4

5. Serve soup with Parmesan cheese.

Cook's Notes

TIME: Preparation takes about 10 minutes, cooking takes about 1 hour.

COOK'S TIP: Try a combination of hot and regular Italian sausage for added flavor.

SERVING IDEA: This is a hearty main dish soup. Serve with a green salad and garlic toast to complete the meal.

DILLY CREAM APPETIZERS

Makes about 3-4 dozen appetizers

The fresh taste of lemon and the distinctive taste of dill add up to a yummy combination with shrimp.

⅓ cup Heinz Tomato Ketchup
1 package (3 oz) cream cheese, softened
1 tsp lemon juice
½ tsp dried dill weed
¼ tsp grated lemon peel
Dash garlic powder
2 to 3 small zucchini, sliced ¼-inch thick
36 to 48 small to medium cooked shrimp, chilled

1. For dressing, thoroughly combine ketchup, cream cheese, lemon juice, dill, lemon peel and garlic powder.

2. Cover and chill to blend flavors.

3. Spoon or pipe a small amount of dressing on each zucchini slice. Top with shrimp. Garnish with fresh dill, if desired.

STEP 3

STEP 1

STEP 3

Cook's Notes

⏱ TIME: Preparation takes about 10 minutes plus chilling time.

🍳 COOK'S TIP: Substitute fresh dill for the dried dill if it is available. Use 1½ teaspoons snipped fresh dill in place of the dried dill for a fresher taste and brighter color.

❓ VARIATION: Cooked, chilled tortellini can be substituted for the shrimp.

◣ PREPARATION: Soften cream cheese quickly in the microwave oven. Unwrap cheese and place in a microwave-safe bowl. Microwave at HIGH 10 to 15 seconds.

APPETIZING KABOBS

Makes about 1 cup sauce

Different combinations of fruits and vegetables can be used with this simple ketchup mixture to make this recipe your own. Try substituting pork or ham for the chicken.

Skinless boneless chicken breast cubes (about ¾ inch)
Bacon slices, partially cooked, quartered
Whole water chestnuts
Red apples, cut into chunks
Firm pears, cut into chunks
¾ cup Heinz Tomato Ketchup
2 tbsp honey
1 tbsp Dijon-style mustard

1. Soak round wooden toothpicks in water for 10 minutes.

2. Thread toothpicks with chicken, bacon, water chestnut and fruit.

STEP 1

3. Combine ketchup, honey and mustard.

STEP 3

4. Brush each kabob generously with ketchup mixture.

5. Place on lightly oiled broiler pan.

6. Broil, 3 to 4 inches from heat source, for 3 to 4 minutes. Turn and brush with sauce.

STEP 6

7. Broil an additional 3 to 4 minutes or until chicken is cooked.

Cook's Notes

⏲ TIME: Preparation takes 10 minutes, cooking takes about 10 minutes.

❗ WATCHPOINT: Be certain that each kabob is completely covered with ketchup mixture before broiling.

🍳 COOK'S TIP: This recipe can be adapted to make a main meal entrée. Use large skewers and add vegetables such as mushrooms, peppers and zucchini to the kabobs. Increase the amount of sauce proportionally.

CRANBERRY SAUCED CHICKEN

Serves 4

It is easy to keep fat and calories under control with simple-to-prepare recipes like this one.

4 skinless boneless chicken breast halves (about 1 pound)
2 tsp vegetable oil
½ cup Heinz Tomato Ketchup
⅓ cup cranberry juice cocktail
⅓ cup fresh or frozen cranberries
¼ tsp allspice
2 tsp cornstarch
1 tsp granulated sugar
⅛ tsp salt
Dash pepper

1. In large skillet, brown chicken in oil; drain excess fat.

STEP 1

2. Thoroughly combine ketchup, cranberry juice, cranberries, allspice, cornstarch, sugar, salt and pepper, stirring to dissolve cornstarch and sugar.

3. Pour over chicken. Cover and simmer 4 minutes, stirring occasionally.

STEP 3

4. Turn chicken and simmer an additional 4 minutes or until chicken is tender.

Microwave Directions: Omit vegetable oil. Place chicken in 1½-quart oblong baking dish and cover with waxed paper. Microwave at HIGH 6 to 8 minutes, turning chicken over and rearranging halfway through cooking. Keep warm. In 2-cup glass measure, combine ketchup, cranberry juice, cranberries, allspice, cornstarch, sugar, salt and pepper. Microwave at HIGH 2 to 3 minutes until thickened and bubbly, stirring twice. Serve sauce over chicken.

Cook's Notes

TIME: Preparation takes 5 minutes, cooking takes about 15 minutes.

SERVING IDEA: Serve with your favorite seasonal vegetables and long grain and wild rice.

COOK'S TIP: Buy fresh cranberries when they are in season and freeze them for later use. Stem, sort, pack in plastic bags and freeze for a fresh cranberry taste all year round.

CHICKEN PIZZAIOLA
Serves 4

Chicken with an herbed tomato-cheese topping "in the style of pizza" is sure to be a hit with big folks and little ones.

4 skinless boneless chicken breast halves (about 1 pound)
1 egg, well beaten
⅓ to ½ cup seasoned dry bread crumbs
2 tbsp butter or margarine
¼ cup Heinz Tomato Ketchup
¼ tsp dried oregano leaves, crushed
2 tbsp grated Parmesan cheese
4 slices (1 oz each) mozzarella cheese

1. Flatten chicken breasts to ¼-inch thickness.

2. Dip each breast in egg, then coat well with crumbs.

STEP 2

3. Slowly sauté chicken in butter until lightly browned on both sides and chicken is cooked.

4. Combine ketchup and oregano and spoon 1 tablespoon mixture over each breast.

STEP 4

5. Sprinkle with Parmesan cheese and place mozzarella on top.

STEP 5

6. Cover, and heat about 2 to 3 minutes until cheese is melted.

Cook's Notes

⏱ TIME: This entrée is quick and easy – it can be prepared and cooked in less than 15 minutes.

? VARIATION: One cup of shredded mozzarella cheese can be used in place of slices.

◯ SERVING IDEA: Serve with hot buttered noodles or pasta and a green vegetable such as broccoli.

BARBECUED CHICKEN WINGS BAHAMA

Makes about 20 appetizer pieces

Chicken wings with a sweet-sour twist. Be sure to make plenty – everyone will love them.

2 pounds chicken wings (about 10)
⅔ cup Heinz Tomato Ketchup
2 tbsp lime juice
1 tbsp brown sugar
½ tsp allspice
¼ tsp red pepper
⅛ tsp garlic powder

1. Cut off wing tips and discard; cut each wing in half at joint.

STEP 1

2. Place wings on broiler rack. Bake in 400°F oven 40 minutes, turning once.

3. Meanwhile, combine ketchup, lime juice, brown sugar, allspice, red pepper and garlic powder; brush on wings.

STEP 3

4. Broil 2 to 3 minutes. Turn wings and brush with sauce.

STEP 4

5. Broil an additional 2 to 3 minutes.

Cook's Notes

⏱ TIME: Preparation takes 5 minutes, cooking takes about 50 minutes.

👨‍🍳 COOK'S TIP: Wing tips can be reserved and used for making chicken stock.

❓ VARIATION: The heat in this recipe can be adjusted to taste by increasing or decreasing the red pepper. For even more zip, add a few drops of red pepper sauce.

MEDITERRANEAN CHICKEN

Serves 4-5

In this recipe the flavors of the Mediterranean combine with chicken for a winning taste.

2 to 2½ pounds broiler-fryer chicken pieces
1 tbsp vegetable oil
1 medium onion, sliced
½ cup chopped celery
1 clove garlic, minced
1 cup Heinz Tomato Ketchup
1 cup water
2 tbsp dry red wine (optional)
1 bay leaf
½ tsp Italian seasoning
¼ tsp salt
¼ tsp pepper

1. In large skillet, brown chicken well in oil; remove. Drain drippings, reserving 1 tablespoon.

STEP 1

2. Sauté onion, celery and garlic in reserved drippings until onion is tender.

STEP 2

3. Stir in ketchup, water, wine, bay leaf, Italian seasoning, salt and pepper.

4. Add chicken and baste with sauce.

STEP 4

5. Cover and simmer 35 to 45 minutes or until chicken is tender, basting occasionally.

6. Remove bay leaf and skim excess fat from sauce.

7. Thicken sauce with mixture of equal parts flour and water, if desired.

Cook's Notes

⏲ TIME: Preparation takes 15 minutes, cooking takes 35 to 45 minutes.

👨‍🍳 COOK'S TIP: Italian seasoning is a blend of oregano, marjoram, basil, thyme, savory, rosemary and sage.

◯ SERVING IDEA: Serve chicken and sauce with pasta or noodles and a mixed green salad.

❗ WATCHPOINT: Chicken breast meat cooks more quickly than dark meat. If cooking a combination of white and dark meat, test white meat at the minimum time and remove if cooked. Dark meat may require an additional 5 to 10 minutes.

SWEET AND SPICY GLAZED CHICKEN

Serves 4-5

This spicy fruit glaze perks up the taste of chicken.

⅔ cup Heinz Tomato Ketchup
2 tbsp apricot preserves
1 tbsp pineapple preserves
2 tsp prepared mustard
½ tsp ginger
¼ tsp cardamom
⅛ tsp garlic powder
2 to 2½ pounds broiler-fryer chicken pieces

STEP 2

1. Combine ketchup, apricot preserves, pineapple preserves, mustard, ginger, cardamom and garlic powder; set aside.

3. Remove skin if desired.

4. Brush chicken with reserved sauce and broil 5 minutes.

STEP 1

STEP 4

2. Broil or grill chicken 35 to 40 minutes, turning once.

5. Turn chicken, brush with sauce and broil an additional 5 minutes.

Cook's Notes

🕐 TIME: Preparation takes 5 minutes, cooking takes about 50 minutes.

❓ VARIATION: Try this fruity glaze on chicken kebabs, pork chops or ham.

◻ SERVING IDEA: Serve chicken with a fresh, crisp salad.

🍴 COOK'S TIP: The use of a hot, zesty prepared mustard will give more spark to this glaze. There are many varieties from which to choose – try the tangy Dijon, hot German or English mustards. Chinese mustards are usually the hottest and most pungent.

MEXICAN MOSAIC CHICKEN
Serves 6

The onions, olives and cheeses add eye appeal as well as flavor to this quickly-prepared chicken dish.

6 skinless boneless chicken breast halves (about 1½ pounds)
1 tbsp vegetable oil
¾ cup Heinz Tomato Ketchup
1 can (4 oz) chopped green chilies, drained
¼ cup thinly sliced green onions
¼ cup sliced pimiento-stuffed or ripe olives
½ cup shredded Monterey Jack cheese
½ cup shredded Cheddar cheese
2 tbsp chopped cilantro or parsley

1. Flatten chicken to ¼-inch thickness.

STEP 1

2. In large skillet, lightly brown chicken in oil. Place in shallow baking pan.

3. Combine ketchup, chilies and onions; spoon ketchup mixture on each chicken piece.

STEP 3

4. Bake in preheated 350°F oven, 15 minutes.

5. Top with olives and cheese and bake an additional 10 minutes.

STEP 5

6. Garnish with cilantro or parsley before serving.

Cook's Notes

🕐 TIME: Preparation takes 5 minutes, cooking takes about 30 minutes.

👨‍🍳 COOK'S TIP: Heat level can be increased by adding a bit of chopped jalapeno pepper or other hot peppers to the ketchup mixture.

◼ PREPARATION: Flatten chicken breasts by pounding with a meat mallet or small skillet, or rolling with a rolling pin.

◻ SERVING IDEA: Serve with parsleyed new potatoes, crisp green salad and biscuits or seeded rolls.

CORAL CREAM SHRIMP

Serves 4

Shrimp and cucumber team up for an unusual flavor combination in this gently seasoned main dish.

1 medium cucumber
2 tbsp butter or margarine
1 cup milk
1 pound raw shrimp, shelled, deveined
¼ cup julienne pimiento
½ tsp salt
⅛ tsp pepper
1½ tbsp cornstarch
3 tbsp water
¼ cup Heinz Tomato Ketchup
3 tbsp dry sherry (optional)
Hot cooked rice

1. Peel cucumber, split lengthwise and remove seeds. Cut into strips 2 inches long.

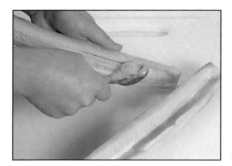

STEP 1

2. Sauté cucumber in butter 1 minute.

3. Stir in milk and heat to simmering.

4. Add shrimp, pimiento, salt and pepper.

STEP 4

5. Combine cornstarch and water and stir into milk mixture.

6. Cook until mixture is thickened, stirring occasionally.

7. Blend in ketchup and sherry. Simmer, uncovered, 5 minutes, stirring occasionally.

STEP 7

8. Serve over rice.

Cook's Notes

⏱ TIME: Preparation takes 5 minutes, cooking takes about 10 minutes.

❓ VARIATION: One package (12 oz) shelled, deveined frozen shrimp, thawed, may be substituted.

❗ WATCHPOINT: Shrimp is cooked when it turns pink. Do not overcook as it will become tough.

⊙ SERVING IDEA: Serve with steamed green beans and a fresh fruit salad.

👨‍🍳 COOK'S TIP: Cooking time is for medium shrimp. If shrimp are larger or smaller, adjust cooking time accordingly.

CATFISH ITALIANO

Serves 4

A low-fat alternative to fried fish, yet simple to prepare and very tasty.

⅓ cup dry bread crumbs
2 tbsp grated Parmesan cheese
¼ tsp garlic powder
¼ tsp salt
⅛ tsp pepper
4 catfish fillets (about 5 oz each)
2 tbsp lemon juice
Nonstick cooking spray
½ cup Heinz Tomato Ketchup
¼ tsp dried oregano leaves, crushed
¼ tsp dried basil leaves, crushed
⅛ tsp hot pepper sauce
¼ cup shredded part-skim mozzarella cheese

1. Combine bread crumbs, Parmesan cheese, garlic powder, salt and pepper.

2. Dip fish in lemon juice, then coat both sides with crumb mixture.

3. Place fish in a shallow baking pan that has been coated with cooking spray.

4. Bake, uncovered, in 400°F oven, 10 minutes.

5. Meanwhile, combine ketchup, oregano, basil and hot pepper sauce.

STEP 2

6. Spoon ketchup mixture over fish and sprinkle with mozzarella cheese.

STEP 6

7. Bake an additional 5 minutes or until fish is cooked.

Cook's Notes

⏱ TIME: Preparation takes 10 minutes, cooking takes about 15 minutes.

👨‍🍳 COOK'S TIP: Catfish are fresh water fish that are now being farm-raised, making them widely available. This firm, mild-flavored fish is low in fat.

◯ SERVING IDEA: Rice pilaf and fresh vegetables will complete this healthy-eating meal.

❓ VARIATION: Other types of firm mild-flavored fish may be substituted. Increase cooking time slightly for thicker fish.

PORK CHOPS PROVENCAL

Serves 4

A savory blend of vegetables and herbs make pork chops special enough for any occasion.

4 rib pork chops, cut 1-inch thick
1 tbsp vegetable oil
1 small eggplant, peeled, diced (about 2½ cups)
¼ cup finely chopped onion
¼ cup chopped celery
1 clove garlic, minced
½ cup Heinz Tomato Ketchup
¼ cup water
¼ cup sliced, ripe olives
1 tbsp drained capers
1 tsp Heinz Vinegar
¼ tsp salt
¼ tsp dried oregano leaves, crushed
¼ tsp dried basil leaves, crushed
¼ tsp pepper

1. In a large skillet, quickly brown chops in oil; remove.

2. Drain drippings, reserving 2 teaspoons.

3. Sauté eggplant, onion, celery and garlic in reserved drippings until tender.

STEP 3

4. Stir in ketchup, water, olives, capers, vinegar, salt, oregano, basil and pepper.

5. Cover and simmer 10 minutes.

6. Return chops to skillet and simmer, covered, 15 minutes, turning once.

STEP 1

STEP 6

Cook's Notes

⏱ TIME: Preparation takes 5 minutes, cooking takes 30 to 35 minutes.

👨‍🍳 COOK'S TIP: Today's pork is lighter and leaner than ever and cooks more quickly.

Overcooking robs pork of tenderness, juiciness and flavor.

○ SERVING IDEA: Serve with rice pilaf, a simple Bibb lettuce salad and crusty bread.

TURKEY CHILI

Serves 10-12

Another healthy choice recipe, this chili sacrifices some of the fat but none of the taste.

2 pounds ground, raw turkey
1 tbsp vegetable oil
1 cup chopped onions
1 cup chopped celery
1 cup chopped green pepper
2 cloves garlic, minced
2 cans (14½ oz each) tomatoes, cut into bite-size pieces
1 can (8 oz) tomato sauce
1 cup water
½ cup Heinz Tomato Ketchup
1 tbsp chili powder
1 tsp cumin seeds
1 tsp salt
½ tsp dried basil leaves, crushed
¼ tsp red pepper
2 cans (15½ to 17 oz each) red kidney beans, drained

1. In Dutch oven, cook turkey in oil 5 minutes or until no longer pink, stirring to crumble. Remove turkey with slotted spoon.

2. Sauté onion, celery, green pepper and garlic in drippings until tender.

3. Stir in turkey, tomatoes, tomato sauce, water, ketchup, chili powder, cumin, salt, basil and red pepper.

STEP 3

4. Cover and simmer 1 hour, stirring occasionally.

5. Add kidney beans and simmer an additional 15 minutes.

STEP 5

6. Serve in bowls, topped with shredded Cheddar cheese and sliced green onions, if desired.

Cook's Notes

TIME: Preparation takes 10 minutes, cooking takes about 1½ hours.

PREPARATION: Ground turkey is used in place of ground beef in this tasty chili recipe. Turkey adds great flavor and is lower in fat.

VARIATION: Chili powder is a blend of dried chilies and other seasoning. If you like a zippy chili, increase the amount or use a brand that is hotter.

SERVING IDEA: Serve Turkey Chili with taco chips.

ORANGE BARBECUED SPARERIBS

Serves 4

A summertime favorite brushed with a citrus-spice glaze.

---

3 to 4 pounds spareribs
Salt and pepper
1 cup Heinz Tomato Ketchup
2 tbsp frozen orange juice concentrate, thawed
1 tbsp honey
1 tbsp grated orange peel
½ tsp dry mustard
¼ tsp ginger
⅛ tsp garlic powder

---

1. Cut ribs into 2 rib sections.

STEP 1

2. Place ribs in large pot with enough water to cover and parboil until tender – about 40 minutes. Drain well and season with salt and pepper.

3. Combine ketchup, orange juice concentrate, honey, orange peel, dry mustard, ginger and garlic powder; brush on both sides of ribs.

STEP 3

STEP 3

4. Grill or broil 6 inches from heat source until ribs are hot, about 6 to 7 minutes per side, brushing frequently with sauce.

Cook's Notes

⏱ TIME: Preparation takes 5 minutes, cooking takes about 1 hour.

🍞 COOK'S TIP: Ribs may be cooked ahead of time. Refrigerate, covered, until ready to use. Warm slightly before brushing with barbecue sauce.

❓ VARIATION: The orange barbecue sauce can also be used in pork chops and chicken.

◣ PREPARATION: Braising or parboiling ribs before grilling helps rid them of excess fat so they are less likely to cause flare-ups on the grill.

BEEF PATTIES WITH PICADILLO SAUCE

Serves 5

A favorite in many Spanish-speaking countries, Picadillo Sauce adds a unique flavor to ground beef.

1 cup Heinz Tomato Ketchup
½ cup finely chopped onion, divided
¼ cup raisins
3 tbsp water
1 tbsp chopped green chilies
1 tsp granulated sugar
½ tsp cinnamon
⅛ tsp ground cumin
1½ pounds lean ground beef
⅓ cup Heinz Tomato Ketchup
1 tbsp Heinz Worcestershire Sauce
½ tsp garlic salt
¼ tsp pepper
¼ cup toasted sliced almonds

1. In small saucepan, combine the 1 cup ketchup, ¼ cup onion, raisins, water, chilies, sugar, cinnamon and cumin.

STEP 2

2. Simmer 5 minutes; set aside.

3. Combine beef, the ⅓ cup ketchup, the remaining ¼ cup onion, Worcestershire sauce, garlic salt and pepper; form into 5 patties.

STEP 3

STEP 5

4. Grill or broil 4 to 5 minutes per side or to desired doneness.

5. Stir almonds into sauce just before serving over beef patties.

Cook's Notes

TIME: Preparation takes about 15 minutes, cooking takes 10 minutes.

VARIATION: Picadillo sauce is equally good served over grilled or broiled steaks or lamb chops.

PREPARATION: Sauce may be prepared ahead of time. To serve, reheat and stir in almonds.

HIGHLAND POT ROAST
Serves 6-8

The traditional flavors of pot roast are enhanced with the addition of apricots and ketchup.

2 to 2½ pounds beef eye of round roast or boneless pork loin
2 tbsp vegetable oil
8 small potatoes, peeled
4 medium carrots, quartered
2 ribs celery, cut into 2-inch pieces
1 tsp salt
⅛ tsp pepper
16 dried apricots
1 cup Heinz Tomato Ketchup

1. In Dutch oven, brown meat in oil.

2. Arrange potatoes, carrots and celery around meat and season with salt and pepper.

STEP 2

3. Place apricots on top of meat and pour ketchup over all.

STEP 3

4. Cover and bake in 325°F oven for 2½ to 3 hours, basting occasionally, until meat and vegetables are tender.

STEP 4

Cook's Notes

⏱ TIME: Preparation takes about 10 minutes, cooking takes 2½ to 3 hours.

👨‍🍳 COOK'S TIP: Leftover meat can be used in casseroles or in sandwiches.

❓ VARIATION: One cup sliced fresh mushrooms may be substituted for the apricots.

🔷 BUYING GUIDE: Look for roasts with little or no fat. If desired, any fat can be trimmed easily with a sharp knife before cooking.

⬭ SERVING IDEA: This is a one-pot meal. A crisp green salad is all that is needed for a well-balanced meal.

GLAZED TOP MEAT LOAF
Serves 6

The perennial favorite dressed up with a glazed top.

⅓ cup Heinz Tomato Ketchup
¼ cup water
1 cup soft bread crumbs
1½ pounds lean ground beef
2 eggs, slightly beaten
2 tbsp minced onion
1 tsp salt
⅛ tsp pepper
¼ cup Heinz Tomato Ketchup
2 tbsp pancake syrup

1. In small bowl, combine the ⅓ cup ketchup and water; stir in bread crumbs and set aside.

2. In large bowl, combine meat, eggs, onion, salt and pepper; add bread crumb mixture and mix thoroughly.

STEP 2

3. Shape into loaf (8 x 4 x 1½-inches) in shallow baking pan.

STEP 3

4. Bake in 350°F oven, 50 minutes.

5. Meanwhile, combine the ¼ cup ketchup and syrup; spread over top of meat loaf.

STEP 5

6. Bake an additional 10 minutes. Allow meat loaf to stand 5 minutes before slicing.

Cook's Notes

L TIME: Preparation takes about 10 minutes, cooking takes 1 hour.

◤ PREPARATION: To quickly make soft bread crumbs, place fresh bread slices in food processor and process until coarse crumbs are formed. Extra bread crumbs may be frozen for later use.

? VARIATION: Light corn syrup or honey can be substituted for the pancake syrup.

O SERVING IDEA: Serve meat loaf with baked potato and stir-fried vegetables.

PARTY BARBECUES

Makes 12-14 sandwiches

A great party recipe, this can be prepared ahead and reheated at serving time.

3 to 3½ pounds beef brisket
¼ cup water
2 tbsp liquid smoke
1 tsp garlic salt, divided
¼ tsp black pepper
2½ cups Heinz Tomato Ketchup
⅓ cup firmly packed brown sugar
2 tbsp Heinz Worcestershire Sauce
1 tbsp Heinz Apple Cider Vinegar
1 tsp prepared mustard
½ tsp onion salt
¼ tsp black pepper
¼ tsp red pepper
Semi-hard rolls or sandwich buns

1. Place beef, water, liquid smoke, ½ teaspoon garlic salt and pepper in Dutch oven.

STEP 1

2. Cover tightly; cook over low heat 2 hours.

3. Remove beef and reserve ½ cup meat juices.

4. Thinly slice beef diagonally across the grain.

STEP 4

5. In same Dutch oven, combine reserved meat juices, ketchup, brown sugar, Worcestershire sauce, vinegar, mustard, the remaining ½ teaspoon garlic salt, onion salt, black pepper and red pepper.

6. Add sliced beef; heat. Serve in rolls.

STEP 6

Cook's Notes

⏰ TIME: Preparation takes 5 minutes, cooking takes about 2 hours.

👨‍🍳 COOK'S TIP: Chill meat and juices after cooking. The meat will be easier to slice when cold and any excess fat can be removed from the juices.

◤ PREPARATION: The addition of liquid smoke to the cooking liquid gives the beef a "grilled outdoors" flavor.

✳ FREEZING: Any leftovers may be frozen for later use.

FLAVORFUL STEAK STRIPS

Serves 6

If you're cooking for a small family, prepare this dish and freeze a portion for another time.

2 pounds beef round steak, cut ½-inch thick
2 tbsp vegetable oil
1 medium onion, halved, thinly sliced
1 clove garlic, minced
1 cup Heinz Tomato Ketchup
½ cup water
2 tbsp Heinz Vinegar
1 bay leaf
½ tsp salt
½ tsp cinnamon
¼ tsp nutmeg
¼ tsp pepper
⅛ tsp ground cloves
3 tbsp raisins
Hot cooked noodles

1. Thinly slice beef diagonally across grain into ½-inch strips.

2. Heat oil in large skillet. Brown beef in two batches and remove.

3. In same skillet, sauté onion and garlic, adding more oil if necessary.

4. Stir in ketchup, water, vinegar, bay leaf, salt, cinnamon, nutmeg, pepper, cloves and raisins.

STEP 4

5. Add browned beef; cover and simmer 1 hour or until beef is tender, stirring occasionally.

STEP 5

6. Discard bay leaf. Serve beef over noodles.

Cook's Notes

TIME: Preparation takes about 10 minutes, cooking takes 1 hour.

COOK'S TIP: For easier slicing, place round steak in the freezer until it becomes slightly frozen.

SERVING IDEA: A crisp green salad would be a pleasant accompaniment.

WATCHPOINT: Skillet must be hot before adding beef. The addition of too much beef at once will cause the temperature to drop and beef will simmer and lose juices instead of browning.

TANGY TOMATO BEEF

Serves 6

Lighter eating doesn't mean sacrificing hearty flavors. Watch this recipe become a new family favorite.

1½ pounds boneless beef sirloin steak
Nonstick cooking spray
2 cups sliced fresh mushrooms
1 cup chopped onions
2 cloves garlic, minced
½ cup water
1 tsp Heinz Worcestershire Sauce
1 tsp instant beef-flavored granules
¼ tsp dry mustard
¼ tsp pepper
½ cup Heinz Tomato Ketchup
½ cup plain nonfat yogurt
1 tbsp all-purpose flour
3 cups hot cooked noodles
Chopped fresh parsley

1. Cut beef across grain into 2 x ¼-inch strips.

2. Coat large skillet with cooking spray.

3. Quickly brown beef strips in skillet, a few at a time, then remove.

4. Drain drippings from skillet and add mushrooms, onion and garlic.

5. Sauté until onions are tender.

6. Return beef to skillet with any accumulated meat juices.

7. Add water, Worcestershire sauce, beef-flavored

STEP 5

granules, dry mustard, pepper and ketchup; simmer 5 minutes.

8. Combine yogurt and flour and slowly stir into beef mixture.

STEP 8

9. Cook over low heat until thickened, stirring occasionally. Serve over noodles; sprinkle with parsley.

Cook's Notes

⏱ TIME: Preparation takes 10 minutes, cooking takes about 15 minutes.

🍲 COOK'S TIP: Although beef granules dissolve more easily, one beef bouillon cube can be substituted.

◼ PREPARATION: The use of nonfat yogurt instead of sour cream keeps the fat and calories under control while adding a bit of extra tang.

TEXAS BEEF CASSEROLE

Serves 6-8

South of the border flavors give interest to this family casserole.

1 pound lean ground beef
1 cup chopped onions
1 clove garlic, minced
1 can (4 oz) chopped green chilies
½ cup sliced ripe olives
1 tsp chili powder
½ tsp ground cumin
¼ tsp red pepper
1 tbsp chopped fresh cilantro
1 cup Heinz Tomato Ketchup
1 cup milk
2 eggs, beaten
2 cups coarsely crushed corn chips, divided
2 cups shredded Cheddar cheese, divided
1 carton (8 oz) dairy sour cream

1. In large skillet, cook beef with onions and garlic until onions are tender; drain excess fat.

2. Combine beef mixture with chilies, olives, chili powder, cumin, red pepper, cilantro and ketchup; set aside.

3. Combine milk and eggs; set aside.

4. Place 1 cup corn chips in bottom of lightly greased 2-quart oblong baking dish.

5. Layer with half of meat mixture and ¾ cup cheese; pour half of milk mixture over. Repeat layers.

STEP 5

6. Bake in 350°F oven 30 to 40 minutes.

7. Spread sour cream over top; sprinkle with remaining 1 cup corn chips and ½ cup cheese.

STEP 7

8. Bake an additional 5 minutes until cheese is melted. Let stand 5 minutes before serving.

Cook's Notes

TIME: Preparation takes 10 minutes, cooking takes 40 to 45 minutes.

COOK'S TIP: Cilantro is a herb growing in popularity. It is used in Mexican, Indian, Caribbean and Oriental cooking and is sometimes called Chinese parsley. If it is unavailable, fresh parsley can be substituted although it is less flavorful.

VARIATION: Heat level in this casserole can be adjusted by increasing or decreasing the amount of red pepper.

ZUCCHINI LASAGNE OLE

Serves 6

3 medium zucchini, sliced lengthwise ¼-inch thick
1 pound lean ground beef
½ cup chopped onion
1 cup Heinz Tomato Ketchup
1 can (4 oz) chopped green chilies, drained
½ tsp chili powder
¼ tsp ground cumin
¼ tsp garlic powder
1 egg, slightly beaten
¾ cup low-fat cottage cheese
2 tbsp grated Parmesan cheese
2 tbsp chopped fresh parsley
½ cup shredded part-skim mozzarella cheese

1. Blanch zucchini in boiling water 1 minute; drain well and pat dry with paper towels. Set aside.

STEP 1

2. In skillet, brown beef and onion; drain excess fat.

3. Stir in ketchup, chilies, chili powder, cumin and garlic powder.

4. In small bowl, combine egg, cottage cheese, Parmesan cheese and parsley.

5. Arrange half of zucchini in 1-1½ quart oblong baking dish.

6. Top with egg mixture, then half of beef mixture.

STEP 6

7. Layer remaining zucchini and beef mixture.

8. Cover and bake in 350°F oven, 30 minutes. Uncover and sprinkle with mozzarella cheese.

9. Bake an additional 10 minutes. Let stand 10 minutes before serving.

Cook's Notes

⌁ TIME: Preparation takes 10 to 15 minutes, cooking takes about 50 minutes.

❗ WATCHPOINT: Be sure to watch the time when blanching the zucchini – if allowed to remain in the water too long it will become watery when baked.

◯ SERVING IDEA: Serve this dish with corn muffins and a green salad.

TACO SALAD
Serves 4

A main dish salad that will appeal to young and old alike. Let the kids add their own toppings.

1 pound lean ground beef
½ cup chopped onion
¼ cup chopped green pepper
1 clove garlic, minced
1 tbsp chili powder
¼ tsp ground cumin
1 tbsp vegetable oil
½ cup Heinz Tomato Ketchup
1 can (14 to 15 oz) kidney beans in spicy sauce
8 cups torn mixed salad greens
2 tomatoes, coarsely chopped
Prepared hot or mild salsa
Sliced green onions
Sliced pimiento-stuffed olives
Dairy sour cream
Shredded Cheddar cheese
Tortilla chips

1. In large skillet, brown beef; remove. Drain excess fat.

2. Sauté onion, green pepper, garlic, chili powder and cumin in oil until onion is tender-crisp.

3. Return beef to skillet and stir in ketchup and beans.

4. Cover and simmer 10 minutes, stirring occasionally.

5. Meanwhile, divide greens among 4 serving plates.

STEP 3

6. Spoon meat mixture on greens.

STEP 6

7. Top with tomatoes, salsa, green onions, olives, sour cream and cheese, as desired. Serve with tortilla chips.

Cook's Notes

TIME: Preparation takes 10 minutes, cooking takes about 20 minutes.

VARIATION: For variety, try pinto beans or garbanzo beans instead of kidney beans.

COOK'S TIP: There are many commercially prepared salsas available in the supermarket. Experiment with different brands and heat levels to find one that suits your family's taste.

SAUSAGE AND BEAN SUPPER

Serves 4-5

This hearty one-dish meal is sure to win approval when winter winds blow.

½ pound smoked sausage, halved lengthwise,
    sliced ¼-inch thick
½ cup chopped onion
½ cup thinly sliced celery
½ cup thinly sliced carrot
1 clove garlic, minced
1 tbsp vegetable oil
2 cans (14 to 16 oz each) Great Northern beans
1 cup Heinz Tomato Ketchup
2 tbsp brown sugar
¼ tsp dried thyme leaves, crushed
¼ tsp dried basil leaves, crushed
¼ tsp crushed red pepper

1. In skillet, sauté sausage, onion, celery, carrot and garlic in oil until vegetables are tender-crisp.

STEP 1

2. Combine beans, ketchup, brown sugar, thyme, basil and red pepper in 2-quart casserole. Stir in sausage mixture.

STEP 2

STEP 2

3. Bake in 350°F oven, 45 to 50 minutes, stirring occasionally.

Cook's Notes

⏲ TIME: Preparation takes 10 minutes, cooking takes 45 to 50 minutes.

◆ PREPARATION: There are many different sausages available to suit every taste. Choose the type you prefer, whether it is mild, spicy hot or garlicky.

👨‍🍳 COOK'S TIP: Beans are a very good source of dietary fiber. Their high protein content and reasonable cost make them a dietary staple in many parts of the world.

GRILLED FRANKS WITH THREE ONION RELISH

Makes 8-10 sandwiches

Onions and hot dogs are natural partners. Serve this relish at your next cook-out and watch it disappear.

½ cup Heinz Tomato Ketchup
⅓ cup finely chopped white onion
⅓ cup finely chopped red onion
⅓ cup thinly sliced green onion
1 tsp lemon juice
1 tsp granulated sugar
½ tsp grated lemon peel
⅛ tsp dried thyme leaves, crushed
Dash cloves
Dash hot pepper sauce
1 pound frankfurters
8 to 10 frankfurter buns

1. Combine ketchup, onions, lemon juice, sugar, lemon peel, thyme, cloves and hot pepper sauce.

STEP 1

2. Refrigerate for at least 1 hour.

3. Grill or broil frankfurters.

STEP 3

4. Serve frankfurters in buns with relish.

STEP 4

Cook's Notes

TIME: Preparation takes about 10 minutes plus chilling time; cooking takes about 5 minutes.

COOK'S TIP: There are many varieties of sweet onions, with some type such as Bermuda, Spanish or Vidalia being available year round.

VARIATION: This zesty relish is just as tasty on grilled hamburgers, kielbasa or boneless chicken breasts.

WATCHPOINT: The onion flavor in this relish will get stronger on standing so it is best served soon after preparing.

GREEN BEANS WITH ZESTY TOMATO RELISH

Serves 4-6

Fresh green beans topped with this flavorful relish can be served either as a vegetable or salad. It's low in calories and high in taste.

1 small tomato, peeled, seeded, chopped
½ cup finely chopped celery
¼ cup finely chopped green pepper
¼ cup finely chopped onion
1 tsp vegetable oil
¼ cup Heinz Tomato Ketchup
1 tsp Heinz Vinegar
1 tsp granulated sugar
¼ tsp dried basil leaves, crushed
¼ tsp salt
⅛ to ¼ tsp pepper
Dash hot pepper sauce
1 pound fresh green beans, cooked, chilled

1. In small skillet, sauté tomato, celery, green pepper and onion in oil until tender-crisp.

STEP 1

STEP 2

2. Stir in ketchup, vinegar, sugar, basil, salt, pepper and hot pepper sauce.

3. Cook over low heat 5 minutes.

4. Cover and chill thoroughly.

5. Spoon tomato relish over beans and garnish with fresh basil, if desired.

STEP 5

Microwave Directions: Omit oil. Combine all ingredients except green beans in a 1-quart casserole and cover with lid. Microwave at HIGH, 5 minutes, stirring twice. Chill thoroughly.

Cook's Notes

⏱ TIME: Preparation takes 10 minutes, cooking takes about 10 minutes plus chilling time.

🍳 COOK'S TIP: Relish will keep in the refrigerator for 2 to 3 days but the flavor is at its best when freshly prepared.

❓ VARIATION: This zesty relish may be served over asparagus, broiled swordfish or grilled chicken breasts.

GARDEN VEGETABLE SPREAD

Makes about 2½ cups

1 package (8 oz) light cream cheese, softened
¼ cup Heinz Tomato Ketchup
1 tsp lemon juice
¼ tsp salt
¼ tsp white pepper
½ cup finely grated carrot
½ cup finely chopped celery
¼ cup finely chopped green pepper
¼ cup finely chopped onion
Assorted fresh vegetables or crackers

1. In small bowl, blend cream cheese, ketchup, lemon juice, salt and pepper until thoroughly combined.

STEP 1

2. Stir in carrot, celery, green pepper and onion.

STEP 2

3. Cover and chill. Serve with vegetables or crackers.

STEP 3

Cook's Notes

⏱ TIME: Preparation takes about 15 minutes plus chilling time.

🍳 COOK'S TIP: If you do not have white pepper you may substitute black pepper. White pepper has a milder flavor and is less visible.

◯ SERVING IDEA: Light cream cheese contains 25% less fat than regular cream cheese, so serve this spread with crisp raw vegetables and "lighten up",

◆ PREPARATION: Spread can be made one day ahead and refrigerated until serving time.

SURPRISE CHOCOLATE CAKE

Serves 12

If you don't tell what the surprise ingredient is, they'll never guess.

2 cups all-purpose flour
1½ cups granulated sugar
⅓ cup cocoa
1½ tsp baking soda
½ tsp baking powder
½ tsp cinnamon
¼ tsp salt
1 cup milk
½ cup Heinz Tomato Ketchup
½ cup shortening
1 tsp vanilla
2 eggs
Chocolate frosting or confectioners sugar

1. In large mixing bowl, combine flour, sugar, cocoa, baking soda, baking powder, cinnamon and salt.

2. Add milk, ketchup, shortening and vanilla.

3. Beat at low speed with electric mixer until combined.

4. Add eggs and beat at medium speed for 2 minutes.

5. Spread batter evenly in greased and floured 9 x 13-inch baking pan.

STEP 2

STEP 5

6. Bake in preheated 350°F oven, 30 to 35 minutes or until cake tester inserted in center comes out clean.

7. Cool. Frost with your favorite chocolate frosting or dust with confectioners sugar.

Cook's Notes

🕐 TIME: Preparation takes about 10 minutes, baking takes 30 to 35 minutes.

🍳 COOK'S TIP: The "surprise" ingredient is ketchup. This recipe makes a moist cake which is perfectly complemented with a light fluffy chocolate frosting.

❓ VARIATION: Cake batter can also be spread into two greased and floured 8 or 9-inch layer pans. Bake in preheated 350°F oven, 25 to 30 minutes or until cake tester inserted in center comes out clean.

TIC TAC TOE COOKIES

Makes 4½-5 dozen

Peanut butter cookies with a mystery ingredient.

1½ cups sifted all-purpose flour
½ tsp baking soda
½ tsp salt
½ cup butter or margarine, softened
½ cup granulated sugar
½ cup firmly packed brown sugar
¾ cup chunky peanut butter
¼ cup Heinz Tomato Ketchup
1 egg

1. Sift together flour, soda and salt.

2. Cream together butter, granulated sugar, brown sugar and peanut butter until light and fluffy.

STEP 2

3. Add ketchup and egg; mix well.

4. Thoroughly blend flour mixture into peanut butter mixture.

5. Drop by teaspoonfuls onto greased baking sheets. Press cookie flat with fork, making an impression in two directions.

STEP 5

STEP 5

6. Bake in preheated 375°F oven, 8 to 10 minutes or until golden brown. Cool on wire rack.

Cook's Notes

TIME: Preparation takes about 10 minutes, baking takes 8 to 10 minutes.

PREPARATION: To keep fork from sticking to dough when pressing cookie flat, dip in flour.

VARIATION: Creamy peanut butter may be substituted for the crunchy peanut butter.

FREEZING: Cookies freeze well. Store in an airtight container.

FRUITED SPICE CAKE

Serves 12

This moist cake slices and travels well and is a delectable treat for a picnic or brown bag lunch.

2½ cups all-purpose flour
1 tsp baking soda
1 tsp salt
1 tsp cinnamon
1 tsp allspice
½ tsp ground cloves
½ cup shortening
1½ cups granulated sugar
2 eggs
1 cup buttermilk
½ cup Heinz Tomato Ketchup
1 cup coarsely chopped, cooked prunes
Confectioners sugar or Pastel Cream Cheese
    Frosting

Pastel Cream Cheese Frosting
4 oz cream cheese, softened
¼ cup butter or margarine, softened
2 tbsp Heinz Tomato Ketchup
1 tsp vanilla
2½ cups sifted confectioners sugar

STEP 4

STEP 5

1. Combine flour, baking soda, salt, cinnamon, allspice and cloves; set aside.

2. In large mixing bowl, cream shortening and sugar with electric mixer until light and fluffy.

3. Add eggs, one at a time, beating well after each addition.

4. Combine buttermilk and ketchup. Add to creamed mixture alternately with flour mixture, blending well after each addition. Fold in prunes.

5. Spread batter evenly in greased and floured 10-inch tube pan.

6. Bake in preheated 350°F oven, 50 to 60 minutes or until cake tester inserted near center comes out clean.

7. Cool in pan on rack 30 minutes before inverting. When cool, dust with confectioners sugar or frost with Pastel Cream Cheese Frosting. For frosting, beat the cream cheese, butter, ketchup and vanilla until light and fluffy. Gradually add sugar, beating well.

Cook's Notes

TIME: Preparation takes about 15 minutes, baking takes 50 to 60 minutes, and cooling takes 30 minutes.

COOK'S TIP: If buttermilk is not available, remove 1 tablespoon milk from 1 cup of milk and add 1 tablespoon vinegar; allow to stand for 5 minutes.

VARIATION: ½ cup chopped walnuts or pecans can be added to batter with prunes, if desired.

INDEX

Photography by Peter Barry
Recipes prepared and styled by Helen Burdett
Designed by Judith Chant
Edited by Jillian Stewart
Project co-ordination by Hanni Penrose